COOL
DOUGHS, PUTTIES, SLIMES & GOOPS
CRAFTING CREATIVE TOYS & AMAZING GAMES

REBECCA FELIX

Checkerboard Library

An Imprint of Abdo Publishing
abdopublishing.com

ABDOPUBLISHING.COM

Published by Abdo Publishing, a division of ABDO, PO Box 398166, Minneapolis, Minnesota 55439. Copyright © 2016 by Abdo Consulting Group, Inc. International copyrights reserved in all countries. No part of this book may be reproduced in any form without written permission from the publisher. Checkerboard Library™ is a trademark and logo of Abdo Publishing.

Printed in the United States of America, North Mankato, Minnesota

102015
012016

THIS BOOK CONTAINS
RECYCLED MATERIALS

Content Developer: Nancy Tuminelly
Design and Production: Mighty Media, Inc.
Editor: Liz Salzmann
Photo Credits: Mighty Media, Inc., Shutterstock

The following manufacturers/names appearing in this book are trademarks:
20 Mule Team®, Argo®, Craft Smart®, Elmer's®, Market Pantry™, McCormick®, Nice!™, Play-Doh®, Sta-Flo®

Library of Congress Cataloging-in-Publication Data
Names: Felix, Rebecca, 1984- author.
Title: Cool doughs, putties, slimes & goops : crafting creative toys &
    amazing games / by Rebecca Felix.
Other titles: Cool doughs, putties, slimes, and goops
Description: Minneapolis, MN : Abdo Publishing, [2016] | Series: Cool toys &
    games | Includes index.
Identifiers: LCCN 2015033046 | ISBN 9781680780499
Subjects: LCSH: Handicraft--Juvenile literature. | Polymer clay
    craft--Juvenile literature. | Toys--Juvenile literature.
Classification: LCC TT297 .F45 2016 | DDC 745.5--dc23
LC record available at http://lccn.loc.gov/2015033046

CONTENTS

DOUGH, PUTTY, SLIME, AND GOOP

Have you ever played with slime? Squeezed and stretched putty? Have you sculpted with clay? Then you know how much fun it can be to play with squishy substances!

People have been using clay for thousands of years. It has been used to create homes, weapons, tools, and pottery. People also played

with clay just for the fun of it!

Many squishy substances are now sold around the world. They are called clays, goops, slimes, putties, and doughs. Some of these substances glow in the dark. Others are super gooey, glittery, or even scented!

GOBS OF GOOPS

In the 1990s, the company Nickelodeon made many toy goops and slimes. Gak was a thick, rubbery goop. Floam had tiny foam beads. There was a sandy dough called Zzand and a soft, squishy goop called Skweeez. Nickelodeon also made a watery slime called Goooze and a muddy substance called Smud.

CREATING CLAYS AND GOOPS

Have you wondered what clays and goops are made of? Do you know how they are created? These toys begin with **chemistry**. Every day, toy makers mix ingredients to make fun goops. The way the ingredients react is what makes them gooey, stretchy, or slimy.

The popular toy dough Play-Doh has a soft, smooth **texture**. This is created by the way water and flour interact. Oil and waxy substances keep the dough smooth. But these are just a few ingredients in Play-Doh. The rest are secret. The company also keeps the process for making Play-Doh top secret.

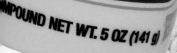

The process for making Silly Putty is not a secret. The ingredients include **boric acid**, silicone oil, powdered fillers, and dry **pigments**. A special machine mixes the ingredients for 30 minutes. Then workers cut the mixture into basketball-sized pieces. The pieces go into the same type of machine used for making **taffy**. The machine cuts the putty into smaller pieces. These pieces are packaged in plastic egg-shaped cases.

BOUNCY BALL

A ball of Silly Putty can **bounce**. But it will break into pieces when hit with a hammer. It can also pick up print from a newspaper!

BECOME A TOY MAKER

THINK LIKE A TOY MAKER

Modern goops and clays come in many different **consistencies**. And they are made in all kinds of colors. Some can even change color!

8

Did you know you can make many of these supercool substances at home?

As you work on the projects in this book, think like a toy maker! Read the steps and look at the photos. Get inspired. Search at home or in craft stores for fun things to add to your goos and putties. Then get creative!

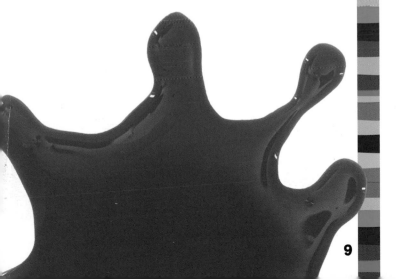

HAVE FUN!

Squeezing and stretching slime, putty, goop, and dough is fun. The process of making toys should be just as fun as playing with them. If something you try doesn't work out, don't worry. Just review the instructions and try again. Get ready to become a toy maker!

MATERIALS

acrylic paint

baking sheet

borax

cornstarch

food coloring

food extract

funnel

gelatin powder

glitter

glow-in-the-dark powder

iron oxide powder

liquid starch

magnetic wand

mason jars

measuring
cups & spoons

mixing bowls

neodymium
magnets

paint
stir stick

plastic zipper bags

Play-Doh

white
all-purpose
glue

SAFETY SYMBOLS

Some projects in this book use strong chemicals or hot tools. This means these projects need adult help. You may see one or more safety symbols at the beginning of a project. Here is what they mean:

 HOT

 GLOVES

BLUBBERY BOUNCY PUTTY

MIX UP A RUBBERY PUTTY THAT MAKES FUNNY NOISES!

1 Put on gloves. Pour ½ cup of room-temperature water into a mixing bowl.

2 Add the glue to the bowl. Stir with a paint stir stick.

3 Stir in a few drops of food coloring. Set the bowl aside.

(continued on next page)

MATERIALS

disposable gloves
measuring cup
water
2 mixing bowls
½ cup white
  all-purpose glue

2 paint stir sticks
food coloring
measuring spoons
4 teaspoons borax
mason jar

4 Pour 1 cup of water into the second mixing bowl. Add the borax powder.

5 Stir the mixture with the second stir stick. Stir until all the powder has **dissolved**.

6 Pour the contents of the second bowl into the first bowl.

7 Stir. The mixture will get thicker as your stir it.

8 Soon the mixture will get too thick to stir. Then mix it with your hands. Squeeze, push, and pull the putty for 10 to 15 minutes. It will become rubbery.

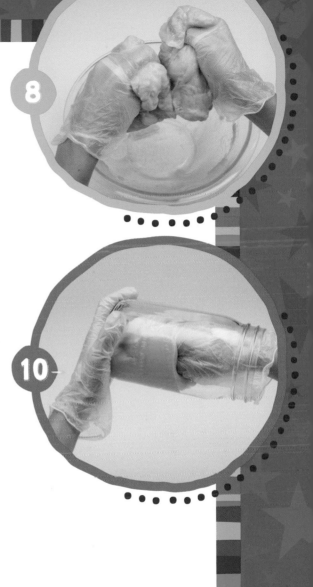

9 **Bounce** your putty on a clean tabletop. Watch the putty bounce and wobble!

10 Push the putty into the bottom of the mason jar. It will make a funny sound!

11 Store the putty in the jar with the lid on. Be sure to wash your hands every time after playing with your Blubbery Bouncy Putty!

MAGNETIC GOOP

MAKE A MYSTERIOUS GOO THAT IS ATTRACTED TO MAGNETS!

1 Put 2 cups water and the borax in a mixing bowl.

2 Stir the ingredients until the borax has **dissolved**. Set the bowl aside.

3 Empty both bottles of glue into the second mixing bowl.

(continued on next page)

CAUTION!

The magnets for this project are very strong! Be careful when separating them so your fingers don't get pinched.

MATERIALS

measuring cup
water
measuring spoons
1 teaspoon borax
2 mixing bowls
paint stir stick
2 4-ounce bottles white all-purpose glue
funnel

disposable gloves
4 teaspoons iron oxide powder
baking sheet
magnetic wand
several neodymium magnets of various sizes
mason jar

4 Some glue will be left inside the bottles. Use a funnel to pour ½ cup of water into each bottle. Put the caps back on and shake the bottles. Then open the bottles and pour the contents into the bowl of glue.

5 Stir the glue and water mixture.

6 Pour the borax mixture into the glue mixture. Stir them together. Keep mixing until the two substances are fully combined.

7 Put on the gloves. Sprinkle the iron oxide onto the mixture. Fold it into the goop. Add ½ cup water and mix with your hands until blended. Place the goop on the baking sheet.

8 Put the small magnets on the magnetic wand. Slowly wave the magnets over the goop. The goop should move toward the magnets!

9 Store the goop in the mason jar. Keep the magnets on top of the lid.

GLOW-IN-THE-DARK GALAXY GOO

MIX UP A STRETCHY, SLIMY DOUGH THAT SPARKLES AND GLOWS!

MATERIALS

- measuring cup
- 1 cup white all-purpose glue
- mixing bowl
- measuring spoons
- 1 tablespoon glow-in-the-dark powder
- paint stir stick
- gel food coloring
- 1 tablespoon liquid starch
- disposable gloves
- glitter
- plastic zipper bag

1 Put the glue in the mixing bowl. Stir in the glow powder.

2 Add a few drops of food coloring and the liquid starch. Stir until well mixed.

3 Put on the gloves. Sprinkle glitter on the mixture. Mix it in with your hands. Keep mixing until the mixture becomes less slimy and more dough-like.

4 Go into a dark room. Squeeze the goo. Watch the glitter shimmer and glow!

5 Store your Galaxy Goo in the plastic zipper bag.

TRY THIS!

Set the goo in the sun for 10 to 15 minutes. Then take it into a dark room. The sunlight charges the glow powder, making it glow brighter!

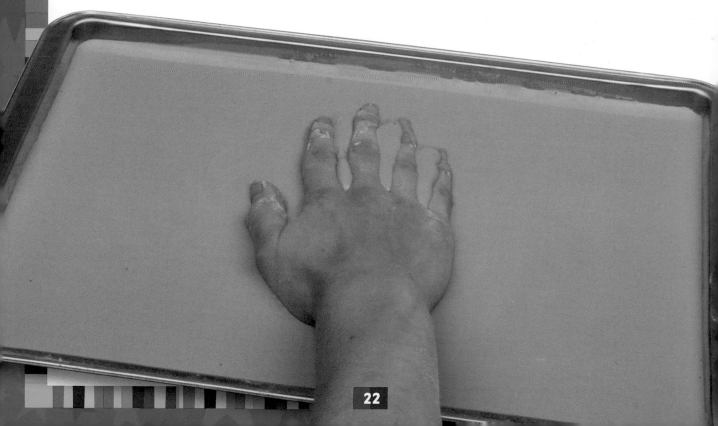

SQUEEZABLE MYSTERY SLIME

AN EASY-TO-MAKE SLIME THAT'S RUNNY AND SOLID AT THE SAME TIME!

1 Put the cornstarch and a few drops of food coloring in the bowl.

2 Slowly add ½ cup water.

3 Put on the gloves. Mix the ingredients with your hands. Add ½ cup of water and mix again.

4 Pour the slime onto the baking sheet. Then squeeze the slime. What does the slime do when you move your hand in it?

5 Store your slime in an airtight container in the refrigerator.

MATERIALS

measuring cups
2 cups cornstarch
food coloring
mixing bowl
water

disposable gloves
baking sheet
airtight container

PLAY-DOH MAZE

CREATE A COLORFUL MAZE
WITH CLAY AND A SHOEBOX LID!

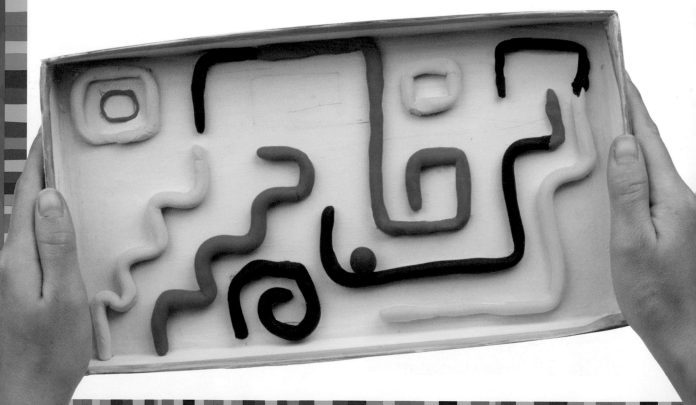

1 Paint the inside of the shoebox lid. Let the paint dry. Then draw a maze inside the shoebox lid.

2 Roll pieces of Play-Doh into shapes that match your maze. Place the Play-Doh shapes over your pencil lines.

3 Make sure the maze is the way you want it. Then glue the Play-Doh shapes in place.

4 Create a Play-Doh ball. Let it and the maze dry for 1 to 2 days.

5 Put the Play-Doh ball in the lid. Tip the lid to roll the ball through your Play-Doh Maze!

MATERIALS

acrylic paint
paintbrush
shoebox lid

pencil
Play-Doh,
  several colors
tacky glue

WORLD-FAMOUS DOUGH

Have you ever used Play-Doh? This dough has been famous for many years! It is known for being soft and smooth. Play-Doh can be used over and over. Or, a Play-Doh figure or shape can be dried. Play-Doh hardens and keeps its shape forever.

This classic dough has come a long way since its invention! Play-Doh was invented by accident. A company called

Kutol Products made a putty to clean wallpaper. In the 1950s, a teacher told an owner of the company that the modeling clay kids used at school was too hard. Kutol Products sent some of its putty to the school to use as clay. It was a hit!

Kutol Products created the Rainbow Crafts Company. The company made a colorful **version** of the putty. This new putty was called Play-Doh. Today, more than 100 million cans of Play-Doh are sold each year.

WHAT'S THAT SMELL?

Play-Doh has a strong scent. It is so well-known that a perfumer made Play-Doh perfume for Play-Doh's fiftieth **anniversary**!

SUPER SCENTED PLAY DOUGH

CREATE PLAY DOUGH THAT SMELLS LIKE ROOT BEER, CHOCOLATE, FRUIT, AND MORE!

1 Put the flour and the salt in a mixing bowl.

2 Choose a scented **extract** or powder for your dough. If you are using an extract, add a few drops to the mixture. If you are using a powder, add about 1 tablespoon.

3 Add a few drops of food coloring if you want colored dough. Keep in mind that some scented extracts and powders will change the dough's color too.

(continued on next page)

MATERIALS

measuring cups
1½ cups flour
½ cup salt
mixing bowls
measuring spoons
food coloring
vegetable oil
water
oven mitts
fork
disposable gloves
plastic zipper bags

SCENTED EXTRACTS AND POWDERS:

banana extract
cherry gelatin powder
cocoa powder
lemon extract
lime gelatin powder
mint extract
orange extract
root beer concentrate
strawberry gelatin powder
vanilla extract

4 Add 1 tablespoon vegetable oil to the bowl.

5 Put 1 cup water in the microwave oven. Heat it on high for 3 to 5 minutes until the water boils. Carefully pour the boiling water into the bowl.

6 Stir the ingredients with the fork. Keep stirring until the mixture thickens into a dough.

7 Put on the gloves. Remove the dough from the bowl. Work the dough with your hands. Add more flour as needed if the dough is too sticky.

8 Repeat steps 1 through 7 to make more scented doughs. Store your doughs in plastic zipper bags.

GLOSSARY

anniversary – the date of a special event that is often celebrated each year.

boric acid – a white acid that contains the metal element boron.

bounce – 1. to spring up or back after hitting something. 2. to throw something down so it hits a surface and springs back up.

chemistry – a science that focuses on substances and the changes they go through.

consistency – how thick, firm, smooth, or sticky something is.

dissolve – to become part of a liquid.

extract – a product made by concentrating the juices taken from something, such as a plant.

pigment – a substance that gives something color.

taffy – a candy usually made with molasses or brown sugar that is boiled and pulled until chewy.

texture – what something feels like, such as rough, smooth, hard, or soft.

version – a different form or type from the original.

WEBSITES

To learn more about Cool Toys & Games, visit **booklinks.abdopublishing.com**. These links are routinely monitored and updated to provide the most current information available.

INDEX